DIGITAL CITIZENSHIP AND YOU™

RESPECTING DIGITAL CONTENT

USING AND SHARING INTELLECTUAL PROPERTY ONLINE

JEFF MAPUA

Rosen
YA™

New York

Published in 2019 by The Rosen Publishing Group, Inc.
29 East 21st Street, New York, NY 10010

Copyright © 2019 by The Rosen Publishing Group, Inc.

First Edition

Library of Congress Cataloging-in-Publication Data

Names: Mapua, Jeff, author.
Title: Respecting digital content : using and sharing intellectual property online / Jeff Mapua.
Description: First edition. | New York, NY : Rosen Publishing Group, Inc., 2019. | Series: Digital citizenship and you | Includes bibliographical references and index.
Identifiers: LCCN 2018021578| ISBN 9781508185260 (library bound) | ISBN 9781508185253 (pbk.)
Subjects: LCSH: Internet and teenagers—Juvenile literature. | Intellectual property—Juvenile literature | Copyright—Juvenile literature. | Plagiarism—Juvenile literature. | Online etiquette—Juvenile literature.
Classification: LCC HQ799.2.I5 M37 2019 | DDC 004.67/80835—dc23
LC record available at https://lccn.loc.gov/2018021578

Manufactured in the United States of America

CONTENTS

INTRODUCTION

Students today live in a much different world from that of their predecessors of a couple decades ago. Before the days of the internet, researching and working on school projects was relatively straightforward. A student would head to the library and find resources to use, whether it be a book, encyclopedia, newspaper, or some other form of media. However, the internet has changed all of that.

Today students must learn the rights and responsibilities of living in a digital world that is interconnected. Books, video files, audio clips, and so much more are available to anyone with an internet connection. As such, students need to engage in ethical and legal behavior while using and sharing this digital content. There are rules and laws in place to protect authors and content creators, and there are ways to safely and legally use their work in research projects and schoolwork.

The internet has provided people with a way to share files in ways that have never been easier. A good digital citizen will know the proper way to use and share intellectual property while respecting the owner's rights. Finally, part of being a good digital citizen is protecting oneself from invasion of privacy online and keeping information accessible online secure.

Respecting digital content and copyright laws could have helped the coffee company Grenade Beverage.

Whether working alone on a project or with a group, it is vital to know what kind of online content you can make use of and how to use it respectfully and legally.

The company entered into an agreement with the Grumpy Cat Limited corporate entity. Grumpy Cat is one of the most enduring memes on the internet, with images of a frowning cat named Tardar Sauce spreading to all digital corners.

While the very nature of memes allows for people to reuse images online, Grumpy Cat Limited handles Grumpy Cat–related licensing for using Tardar Sauce's likeness for consumer products, such as T-shirts, toys, or anything else that people can buy. Grenade Beverage was granted permission to produce and sell Grumpy Cat Grumppuccinos. However, the company pushed the limits of their agreement by also producing and selling Grumpy Cat–branded ground coffee. They did not have permission from Grumpy Cat Limited to make the additional product without their approval.

Grumpy Cat Ltd. sued Grenade Beverage for violating the copyright on their intellectual property. The case was in court for two years and was finally resolved in January 2018. The court awarded Grumpy Cat Ltd. $710,000 in damages. The Grenade Beverage Company failed to demonstrate an understanding of intellectual property. While people are free to share images of Grumpy Cat online, the company ventured into an area that violated copyright, permission, and fair use. There could even be an argument that Grenade Beverage Company engaged in unethical behavior by attempting to profit off of another company's intellectual property. If Grumpy Cat Ltd. decided to produce their own line of coffee, they would have been competing against an unauthorized version of their own intellectual property.

Students today must navigate similar areas of digital rights in their own work. While it may now seem clear that Grenade Beverage was violating their agreement with Grumpy Cat Ltd., it may not always be so clear when it is lawful for students to use images from the internet for their own projects.

CHAPTER ONE

DIGITAL RIGHTS AND INTELLECTUAL PROPERTY

Digital rights and intellectual property are important parts of the creative content found online. They must be respected when used and can cost or earn a company a significant amount of money. However, many people may not know what digital rights are and what counts as intellectual property.

DIGITAL MEDIA

Media are any form or system of communication, entertainment, or information. Traditional examples of media include newspapers, radio, or wired telephones. Digital media are a result of technological advances. The term "digital media" refers to media that come in electronic form or are part of computer technology. For example, radio that is transmitted via the internet is considered digital media, as is a book that can be read using a computer or mobile device. Storage products are also considered digital media. Common examples are CDs, DVDs, MP3 players, and memory sticks.

New types of internet-enabled products, including smartphones and tablets, have challenged the ability of modern researchers and some users to keep up with their capabilities.

An important characteristic of digital media is the ability to be transmitted using computers and networks. Digital content can be distributed to one or more people without having to physically be in the same room. Because of how common and widespread they are, digital media commonly refers to content that can be viewed on a computer or mobile device, such as a phone or tablet.

Sharing digital media goes both ways. One kind of sharing includes sites where viewers can stream movies, music, and other video and audio content. On other sites, users post images or videos online and view other users' photos or videos. One special feature of digital media is the way they bring different people together according to their interests and consumer choices.

WHAT ARE DIGITAL RIGHTS?

The internet enables users to share and copy content quickly and easily. This contrasts with older media formats, especially those used for recording and listening to music and other audio, like compact discs, audio cassettes, and vinyl records. There were ways to copy and distribute these illegally, but we entered an entirely new age when digital files became the norm, more so for music than other media. It became an issue that record labels felt they had to address, lest they be driven out of business. The issue of file sharing—which many considered nothing but online piracy—would soon impact other media, including movies, television shows, music videos, images, and written works.

Digital rights are protected by laws that prevent people from making and distributing unauthorized copies of digital content. Copyright is the legal right of an owner or creator to copy, publish, and sell some form of artistic work. Copyrights protect people from losing money and protect the right to potentially make money from their work in the future. Companies that produce, publish, and sell content have claimed that internet piracy costs them millions annually. The concern is that many people are downloading their content from online sources without paying either the artist or distributor for it.

While people and companies that produce digital material are protected by digital rights, there are also rules in place for the lawful use of content, whether it is compensated (paid for) or not. For example, US law allows for some specific uses of copyrighted material without permission from the copyright owner. These special cases are not considered an infringement of the owner's rights.

Copyright laws and digital rights for students and teachers can get complicated. Michael Moulton, a

For a long time, books and other physically printed content were the only intellectual property covered by existing laws, a situation that changed once the internet was devised.

professor at the University of Florida, sued a company for selling copies of notes his students took in his class. The courts found that some of the sold materials based on his note violated his copyrights, while other materials did not.

WHAT IS INTELLECTUAL PROPERTY?

Intellectual property is everywhere. If someone has ever read a book, looked at artwork or a photograph, watched a television show or movie, read something online, or listened to a song, then that person has enjoyed the intellectual property created by another person or group. A product's name and logo and the jingle the company uses in its commercial to sell their products are considered intellectual property, too. Intellectual property can also include the packaging of a product, like an album or tube of toothpaste. Machines, machine parts, tools, medicines, and hundreds of other items are examples of intellectual property.

Intellectual property is any work or invention that is the result of creativity, to which one has rights and can be legally protected from unauthorized use by other people or groups. The four traditional categories of intellectual property are patent, copyright, trademark, and trade secrets. Intellectual property laws allow inventors and creators to produce goods for the benefit of people while also being properly compensated for their efforts and the end products.

STATUTE OF ANNE

In England, until the early 1700s, a book's copyright was held not by the author but instead by the printer. That means that only the printer could republish written works. The Stationers' Company was a group of printers and publishers, and they held a monopoly over the publishing industry. Authors were not allowed to join. It was thus sometimes considered illegal for an author to self-publish a book.

However, this changed in 1710 with the passage of the Statute of Anne. The statute, named after Queen Anne since it was passed during her reign, gave more rights to authors. The United Kingdom's highest lawmaking body, known as Parliament, paved the way for copyright law for hundreds of years both in the United Kingdom and in the United States, which based many of its precepts on earlier British laws.

THE DIGITAL MILLENNIUM COPYRIGHT ACT (DMCA)

In October 1998, President Bill Clinton signed the Digital Millennium Copyright Act of 1998, or DMCA, into law. In addition to complying with international law, the DMCA addressed copyright issues introduced with the internet.

The law protected companies that provide internet access to people who infringe on copyrighted materials online. This means that if a person were to illegally copy a digital file online, the company that provides internet service to that person will not be held responsible if they follow the law's procedures. They were, however, responsible for disabling access to content that infringed on copyrights and taking down offending websites when required to do so by the law.

One type of service that has largely replaced both illegal and legal file sharing and downloading is the streaming music app.

DMCA also set up protections for people who have been wrongfully accused of copyright infringement. There are specific procedures to follow and conditions that must be met to qualify for this protection. For example, people are required to submit a written statement of innocence, as well as alert the copyright holder. Those making repairs to equipment are also protected if, in the process of fixing an electronic device, they make a copy of copyrighted materials.

Special copyright rules apply for educational nonprofits, faculty, and student employees who are involved in teaching or conducting research. Conditions must be met, including "not providing online access to course materials that were required or recommended during the past three years." The school or institution must also not have received more than two copyright infringement notices in three years.

INTELLECTUAL PROPERTY IN PRACTICE

The DMCA helps protect copyright holders from others using their material without permission. It also helps those who are falsely accused of copyright violations. One such case occurred in 2007 when the National Football League (NFL) sent a takedown notice to Brooklyn Law School professor Wendy Seltzer. Seltzer, who teaches DMCA and copyright law, posted a YouTube video of a class presentation that included a clip of the copyright notice that the NFL displays during games. She wanted to point out that the NFL did not allow for educational use of their content. She argued that the NFL and other copyright holders often went too far and limited uses of their content that should otherwise be perfectly legal. Seltzer sent a counternotification that the clip was fairly used for educational purposes. In the end, Seltzer's video was restored and the professor gave the NFL professional advice. She let the NFL know that they should have sent a court order to keep the video offline instead.

In another example, Stephanie Lenz posted a video on YouTube of her eighteen-month-old son dancing to a song by Prince called "Let's Go Crazy." Lenz was sent a DMCA takedown notice by Universal Music Group for unauthorized use of the song. Lenz sent a

Copyrighted content is all around us, even if we don't realize it. For example, there are often strict rules about recording and showing certain broadcasts.

counternotification claiming that the song played in the background and was unrecognizable in certain parts of the video. She said she was clearly not breaking any laws and that Universal Music Group sent the notice in bad faith. Lenz was eventually supported by the courts and her video was restored online.

CHAPTER TWO

UNDERSTANDING RIGHTS

Copyright and intellectual property rules can be intimidating for those who have no experience with them. For example, not everyone may know the difference between a patent and a trademark, but infringing on either can land someone in hot water. In

addition to learning about the differences, there are also common misconceptions that can confuse youth and laypeople, especially those who are not lawyers, professional artists, or content creators.

COPYRIGHTS

The United States Patent and Trademark Office (USPTO), based in Alexandria, Virginia, is pictured here.

According to the United States Patent and Trademark Office, copyrights are used for literature, drama, music, and artwork. Examples include poetry, books, movies, songs, computer applications, video games, and architecture. A copyright protects original works of creative output or authorship. They do not cover entire subjects, such as math or history, but only creative works. For example, a copyright does not cover the Civil War as a topic, but does protect a particular book written about it. Similarly, copyrights do not protect facts or ideas, but instead protects how those facts or ideas are expressed.

Not all copyrights last the same amount of time. Some creations are protected for longer than others. The length of time depends on the creator. Individuals who create a piece of artistic work have their work protected for the duration of their lifetime plus an additional seventy years afterward. There are things people can do to extend a copyright or keep it within a family. In general, however, if an author who wrote a book died in 1948, the book would lose its copyright protection in 2018.

Artistic creations created either anonymously or under a fictitious name or pseudonym retain copyright protection for ninety-five years from the date of publication or 120 years from the date of creation, whichever is shorter. This type of protection also applies to works created for hire.

LONG-TERM COPYRIGHT

Some people believe that existing copyright laws allow rights to prevail for much longer than necessary. For example, Rick Flakvinge, the founder of the Swedish Pirate Party, heads a political group that supports online piracy of movies, music, and other digital media. He pondered on Torrentfreak.com, "So why does the monopoly last seventy years after the author's death? I don't know of a single author who keeps writing books after they're dead and buried."

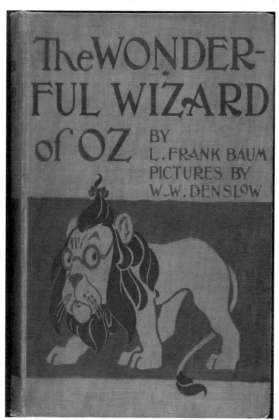

Works in the public domain include Frank L. Baum's children's novel published in 1900, *The Wonderful Wizard of Oz.*

The answer to his question began about seventy years before Flakvinge was born. In 1909, copyrights were mandated to last seventy years. However, this was changed to avoid scenarios in which someone would outlive his or her copyright term. American composer Irving Berlin lived to be 101 years old and would have outlived the copyrights on many of his musical compositions, such as 1942's "White Christmas," among others.

In 1998, the Sonny Bono Copyright Term Extension Act extended all existing copyrights at the time by twenty more years. The Supreme Court denied all challenges to the law, saying that seventy years, while a long period, is still a limited amount of time. The new law was also an attempt to reconcile with another one passed in 1993 by the European Union, or EU. The EU established the copyright term to be life plus seventy years and denied the term to any country that did not abide by the same rules. Passing the Sonny Bono Copyright Term Extension Act ensured that American authors, musicians, and creatives were guaranteed the same protections in Europe as their European counterparts.

REDBOX TAKES ON DISNEY

In late 2017, Disney sued Redbox, a company that operates movie-rental kiosks, or vending machines. Disney claimed that Redbox was violating copyrights by selling movie download codes included in DVD and Blu-Ray purchases that allow people to download a copy of their movies.

In January 2018, Redbox countersued Disney, claiming that the company was misusing copyrights among other illegal activities. Redbox says that Disney is breaking copyright law's first-sale doctrine, which they say allows them to legally obtain copyrighted content to sell. The lawsuits will decide what is included in Disney's copyright while also determining what movie rental and streaming services can and cannot do.

Copyright supporters believe that the laws are intended to protect more than just a single author or musician. According to Stephen Carlisle, a copyright officer at Nova Southeastern University, copyrights are also intended to protect businesses and the people they employ. For example, Carlisle points out that the Walt Disney Company employs hundreds of thousands of people worldwide. Walt Disney World employs more people on one site than any other company in the United States. If Disney's intellectual property were not protected, it is possible that people's jobs could be put in jeopardy.

PATENTS

According to the United States Patent and Trademark Office, a patent is specifically for inventions, machines, manufactured articles, industrial processes, and chemical compositions. A design patent covers the design elements of an invention or product. These are the parts of a product designed to make it pleasing to the eye but are not really connected to its functionality.

Meanwhile, a utility patent is for the functional part of a product. It covers processes, machines, compositions, or uses. Design patents last fifteen years while utility patents last twenty years. Patents can also be extended beyond the original terms. There is a third type of patent called a plant patent. It protects plants that reproduce by grafting or cloning rather than traditional means. While students may not be at risk of infringing a utility patent in standard schoolwork, they could be vulnerable to infringing on design patents.

TRADEMARKS

Trademarks are used to protect a word, phrase, symbol or design that is identified with one business, company, or other party's products or goods. Similar to trademarks are service marks, which identify and distinguish a service instead of a product or good. Common uses of a trademark or service mark are for a brand name, slogan, or logo. Popular slogans include Just Do It for Nike,

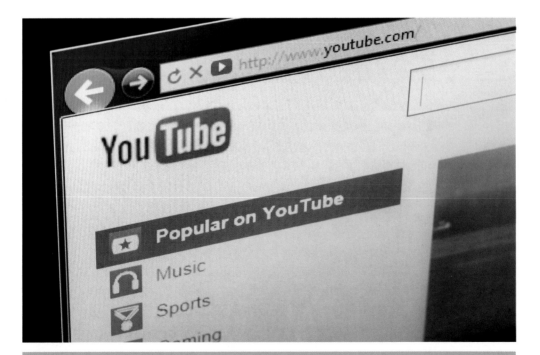

YouTube has very specific guidelines on what kind of content both professionals and amateurs can post if the rights to that content do not technically belong to them.

Think Different for Apple, and I'm Lovin' It for McDonalds. A logo for those companies would be the swoosh, apple, and golden "M" respectively.

Trademarks are different from patents and copyrights in that they can last forever as long as they continued to be used. Trademarks are marked with a "TM" after a symbol or mark, while service marks are marked with an "SM." If a trademark is registered with the United States Patent and Trademark Office, it is marked with a registered symbol, which is the capital letter "R" inside a circle. Students should be careful when using a trademarked slogan or logo in their work. This works the other way around, too: don't put a trademark on something you wrote unless it really and truly is trademarked.

RIGHTS MISCONCEPTIONS

There are limits to what kinds of intellectual property are protected and to what extent. Not everyone is well versed in the ins and outs of this. The NFL experienced this firsthand when it went after the Brooklyn professor and lost in court. Understanding copyright limits protects not only the intellectual property but also its owners from overstating their rights.

One of the most common areas of digital rights concerns copying content for private and noncommercial purposes. The laws are different in various countries. In the United States, some private uses of copied material are acceptable. One such use is when someone makes a copy of a copyrighted program to make backup software copies. In general, copies are legal if they are intended for nonprofit educational purposes but illegal if intended for commercial purposes, including selling the copies for profit.

The law also takes into account the nature of a copyrighted work and how much of that work has been duplicated. A judge will consider if it was just a minor portion of a song or movie or if it was enough to become illegal. If a copy affects the value of the original or has an effect on the potential market for the original, then it could be illegal.

Copyright laws are often complex and can be confusing. It is a branch of the law that demands intense concentration and hard work to master.

In the academic sphere, private copying occurs in various forms. Private-use copying covers hand-copying quotes from a source, such as a book or newspaper, for research purposes. If a student cuts and pastes text from an online or digital source, it is also considered private use if it is intended for research purposes. Some uses, while seen as proper use in academics, are seen by others as infringing on copyrights. These include libraries loaning to other libraries, document delivery in which copies are sent between libraries, and reserving electronic materials for classes. Copyright owners, consumers, students, and teachers all need to have at least a rudimentary knowledge of these issues in many modern media and educational environments.

OTHER MISCONCEPTIONS

There are various misconceptions about copyright law. Anyone posting videos on a website such as YouTube will need to follow copyright law. YouTube grants its users synchronization licenses, meaning a copyright holder does not need to give permission to people who post videos to the site using their media. Instead, the copyright holder gets a share of whatever money the new video makes. However, if a person or band wants to record themselves playing another artist's song, they may need to obtain permission from the rights owner. For rights owners, a copyright exists as soon as the work is completed. However, damages or payback for infringement can only be collected if the copyright is registered with the US

Copyright Office. Another mistake people make is using the DMCA to take down content on the internet that they do not like. The DMCA is only for copyrighted material, not for content someone may find offensive.

Trademarks can be held by someone or a company that did not invent a word, phrase, symbol, or design. For example, the BBC holds a trademark on blue police boxes due to their association with their popular television show *Doctor Who*. Even though the BBC did not invent them, blue police boxes and images of them belong to the BBC. Finally, not selling copied or copyrighted material does not necessarily mean that it is legal. For example, people cannot make copies of a movie and then give it away for free.

CHAPTER THREE

THE INTERNET PROBLEM

While the internet has proven invaluable for students' research options, its advent has also complicated issues surrounding intellectual property and digital rights. Students should have an idea about what they can and cannot do while researching online, using content found there for schoolwork and other uses. Doing so, they can avoid plagiarism, as well as wading into legal trouble with rights holders.

MAKING COPIES

Copyright laws dating back before the internet era were already relatively complicated. The digital realm has complicated things further by adding an international dimension, too. In the United States, intellectual property law has grown over time to adapt to new technology and communications. American users and their international counterparts might have to negotiate several levels of copyright for the same content

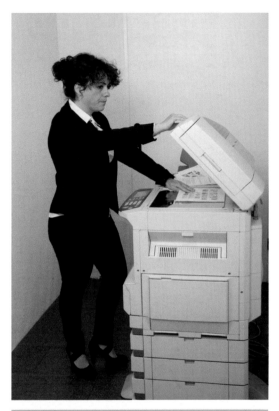

Making physical copies for use by students in class is often okay under copyright law, but it depends on different factors.

across international boundaries and borders.

By design, computers constantly make copies of digital material. To view a web page, for example, a copy of the page is sent to a user's computer from where the page originates. A copy is made on the computer's memory, then a new copy is produced on the computer screen. The same process occurs for digital media such as music and books. All this copying is a headache for rights holders and those in charge of determining what is legal. Coupled with how easy the internet makes it to search, find, and distribute copyrighted material, protecting intellectual property is a major issue today.

RULES FOR SHOWING AUDIOVISUAL WORKS

There are specific rules involved when showing a movie in what could be considered "the public." When someone rents or borrows a movie, that person is free

DIGITAL MEDIA CHARACTERISTICS

Digital copies are not only easy to make, but are, for the most part, usually identical or nearly so, to an original. Unless you are using a high-end stereo or headphones, or are a professional, a duplicated song file will likely sound pretty much like the one being copied.

Compare this to making physical copies of a newspaper. With traditional copy machines, a copy can introduce little mistakes, including blurred portions of a page or slight variations in color or other changes. A copy of a copy introduces more issues, until third- or fourth-generation copies may not resemble the originals at all. Digital media copies, on the other hand, will usually be indistinguishable from source materials in many cases. If a copied MP3, for example, sounded terrible compared to the one that costs $.99 online, one might be inspired to shell out the cash for the latter, instead of downloading the former for free.

Making copies is also relatively cheap. An inexpensive computer, tablet, phone, or other electronic machine can make unlimited copies of digital files. The files themselves can be shrunk or compressed to allow for machines to save a large number of MP3 audio files, videos, books, and more. The combination of inexpensive machines and widespread internet usage represents what some see as a revolution in how content is controlled and maintained.

to watch the movie privately but does not obtain any of the underlying copyrights. If a movie is shown in a nonprivate setting, it could be considered a "public performance," which requires a license from the copyright owner.

The first step in finding out whether or not it is legal to show a movie is determining if it is a public performance or not. Is the movie being shown to people other than family members or a small group of friends? Is the movie being shown in a place open to people other than family members or a small group of friends? If either of these is yes, then it may be considered a public performance. A place "open to people" can be a classroom or a theater in a common area, such as a cafeteria or public library.

However, there are still special circumstances that allow for a movie to be shown in these situations. The

Showing movies and other media in public for a large audience involves restrictions, especially if there is any profit made, even if it is generated by side businesses, such as beverage and food sales.

first case is when a movie has been legally obtained, which does not include a movie being recorded from a broadcast, and is being shown for in-person, or face-to-face, teaching. This covers movies shown in a class-room or place devoted to instruction but does not cover e-classrooms, such as a class held online.

Movies on a school's list of approved distributors or filmmakers are also clear of any copyright infringement. These movies are usually preapproved with rights preobtained for showings. Similarly, some movies come with a license for certain noncommercial institutional purposes. Some educational movies, for example, come with such licenses. Movies in the public domain, or

The ways of broadcasting the content and information we have available to us all must be carefully considered by copyright lawyers, governments, and users of that content.

considered as belonging to the public and not subject to copyright, are free to be shown.

AVOIDING YOUTUBE INFRINGEMENT

YouTube is one of the most popular websites in the world, with more than a billion users and a seemingly endless amount of content. With the number of videos available, copyright infringement is a constant issue the website must grapple with.

YouTube is not responsible for the videos that people upload. It protects copyright owners with a system called Content ID. It uses technology to scan videos submitted by a content owner. If a new video is uploaded that matches another video already on the site, YouTube alerts the copyright owner so he or she is aware of potential infringement. The owner can then remove the video's infringing audio, block the video entirely, place ads on the new video to make money from it, or track the video's viewing statistics. YouTube also gives the new video a license from the original owner if he or she allows the video to remain online.

To avoid violating copyrights when uploading to YouTube, the safest thing to do is to upload only completely original videos. Many people add the phrase, "I claim no right to this song/video," thinking that it is enough to protect them from being accused of copyright infringement, but that is not true. Uploading a copyrighted video is a violation whether or not someone puts a disclaimer on the video. Posting to YouTube can be considered making or distributing a copy of original work. Users should be careful when incorporating other videos or music into their videos.

INSTAGRAM

Instagram is a popular photo sharing application mainly for mobile devices. It allows people to quickly and easily share their own photos, but people can also use it to share other people's photos. Instagram does not allow people to post photos of another person's intellectual property and deletes photos that do. They recommend that their users post only images that they own.

Depending on the media platform or mode of transmission, photos of private individuals (including selfies) cannot be used by others without permission.

Instagram makes a point to alert users that they can infringe on others' copyright even if they do not intend to. The same is true even if users give credit to the copyright owner or include a disclaimer that they do not intend to infringe copyrights. Other Instagram misconceptions about what protects users from infringing on a copyright include saying that a post is fair use, not intending to profit from the post, having purchased content from the internet before posting an image of it, modifying work before posting, finding the content on the internet, recording material—such as music at a concert—on their own device, and posting the same content found elsewhere. Each of these situations is still subject to copyright law.

EDUCATIONAL USE

Educational institutions may use copyrighted material for educational purposes. An educational institution can be a K–12 school, college, university, library, museum, hospital, or other nonprofit institution. As long as they engage in educational and nonprofit instructional, research, or scholarly activities, they will be considered an educational institution.

Educational purposes must be noncommercial in nature. Teachers' instruction of students at a nonprofit educational institution counts as an educational purpose. Another educational purpose is a planned study or investigation meant to contribute to a subject or field of study. Presentations of research or findings at a conference, workshop, or seminar fall under the educational-purpose umbrella, too.

Teachers have specific rules to follow, such as making only one copy of copyrighted material per student and not using copied material in place of texts or workbooks. Teachers can ask for students to pay for copied materials but at a price that only covers the cost of photocopying.

COPYRIGHT AND RESEARCH

Using copyrighted materials even for research purposes may require obtaining permission from the rights owner. Materials found on the internet are not considered in the public domain and are protected by copyright just as printed materials are. There are some things students can do without needing to obtain permission, such as creating links to legally posted material. These links can be used on any website online.

A link is a way for a website to redirect a user from one website or page to another. There are two general types of links. One type takes users from one website to another, completely leaving the first website behind. The other type of link is called an inline link and these bring digital media such as images or audio clips in from another website. This is also called framing since it "frames" one site's content around another. Framing may be considered copyright infringement since it could potentially make one website's content look like it belongs to another.

Reproducing and distributing content found on-line, however, is not always legal without first getting the right to do so. In order for research to be legal and clear of violations, it must be used for nonprofit educational purposes and must transform the work into something new or original.

College students relinquish their copyright ownership for the research they conduct on their own to their institution. A student is considered a member of the staff and all of their work is the property of the university. This also naturally applies whether or not students are employed, either on a part-time or full-time basis, by the university while they study, through work-study programs or otherwise.

Some students form agreements with their university to make money from their research, but such arrangements are far from universal. A research student's intellectual property rights can be claimed and protected by the university since his or her research and work is conducted through that student's association—and sometimes employment—with the university. Each school has different rules and standards, however. Students engaging in research are encouraged to check with their school to determine how their work will be handled under copyright law.

CHAPTER FOUR

PROTECTING DIGITAL RIGHTS

Students should learn how to properly follow copyright rules when conducting research and finding materials online. New technologies have been rolled out in recent years to discourage both those who violate intellectual property rules by accident and intentionally. Such methods are intended to make improper use of intellectual property difficult or impossible. However, not all of them have been welcomed with open arms by rights holders, creators themselves, consumers, or researchers.

TECHNICAL PROTECTION

Technological solutions to protecting intellectual property do not necessarily address whether the laws themselves are good for business and society. They are just a tool to prevent illegal copies from being made of digital media and other copyrighted content. Protection can range from keeping legal owners of copyrighted materials within their legal rights, to keeping other actors, such as online pirates, from duplicating and distributing files such as movies, games, or music.

Technical protection often involves digital media verification. This means that if a digital file, such as a document with important information, has been altered in any way, technology can alert the rights holders or person who purchased the file.

A watermark is a print on an image that tells potential users and researchers that the content is protected.

Designers and programmers have found that adding protection to personal computers is more difficult than on dedicated machines, such as a cable box or MP3 player. Concentrating on hardware is usually more reliable, but measures targeting software are getting more sophisticated now, too.

There are several methods of technical protection. Security and integrity features are found on computer operating systems such as Windows or Apple's macOS. These grant special privileges to access various files on a computer. Encryption takes digital media and makes it unusable to people unless they legally obtain it. For example, an encrypted file will not open on a computer without first verifying that the file was legally purchased. Similarly, rights management languages are instructions that machines can read to allow people to only do what is allowable under copyright law with files.

REGULATION THROUGH LAW

Copyright rules that were created before digital media became widespread are obviously somewhat outdated. The World Intellectual Property Organization adopted the Copyright Treaty in 1996. Among other things, it provided protection for digital media creators from those who broke copyright laws and found ways around technological safeguards.

The United States introduced the Digital Millennium Copyright Act in 1998 that created new laws. Among them include those that made it illegal to find ways around antipiracy measures found in software.

Netflix and other video streaming services and networks pay production companies and other creators for the films and television shows that they offer.

DRM

Digital rights management, or DRM, is technology introduced in the 1990s to help protect intellectual property. One of its biggest uses is to enable secure distribution of digital media. People can safely pass along media that features DRM technology. At the same time, DRM also disables illegal distribution of content over the internet. For example, if someone were to purchase a copy of a song online, he or she could not then share it with another person who has not paid for a copy.

Generally speaking, DRM is a part of every step of the distribution of content online. This includes the description, identification, trading, protecting, monitoring, and tracking of how media is used online. Everything someone does includes DRM.

DRM is about managing digital rights and enforcing the rules. For rights holders, it is their responsibility to identify their content to understand what they really own and assert what rights they have in order to legally distribute it. Rules enforcement is handled by DRM technologies such as secure containers and identification. A secure container is a form of encryption making digital media inaccessible to those not authorized to access it. Identification systems grant access to files to specific people or organizations with proper claims to the digital media.

DRM CONTROVERSY

DRM has allowed artists and computer programmers to control who can view or use their work. DRM can be seen as a digital padlock placed on digital files that requires a special key to open. However, the added copyright security has many people voicing their concerns and issues with the technology.

Since a file's creator ultimately has control over when and how users can use the work, many have pointed out that people never really own what they buy. Critics of DRM say that if someone purchases a digital music file but cannot use and access it as that person wishes, then he or she does not truly own the file.

Some companies have taken drastic measures to protect their software and files. One company, FSLabs, even added a controversial piece of technology to their software. One of the add-ons to a popular flight simulator they produce included a suspicious file. After users investigated the file in early 2018, they discovered that it stole the saved passwords stored in a user's Google Chrome web browser and sent them to the company.

Users were concerned that their private information was vulnerable and confronted the company. FSLabs admitted to including the program that extracted users' saved passwords and usernames. Lefteris Kalamaras, founder and owner of FSLabs, explained that the program was included in an effort to locate the person who originally stole their software and violated their copyrights. Kalamaras said, "We decided to capture his information directly—and only his information." However,

Technologists are busy trying to develop and build new systems that will protect creators, make it easy for users to buy or borrow intellectual property, and accomplish these tasks safely.

FSLabs released an updated version of their software without the offending program. Andrew Mabbitt, founder of cybersecurity company Fidus Information Security, said, "This is by far one of the most extreme, and bizarre, methods of Digital Rights Management we've ever seen."

THE INTERNET AND COPYRIGHT

Copyright laws prevent people from copying and downloading everything they find online for their own use. There are specific rules in place to allow people to use the internet without needing to worry about violating copyright law. For example, even though computers make copies of web pages, such as when a web browser saves a copy so it can load faster in the future, this does not trigger a copyright violation. The copy itself is enough to infringe on copyright, but these copies are acceptable to and expected by the content creator. This is known as implied consent. Anyone who posts something online expects a visitor's computer to make a copy, thus there is an implied license or permission that does not need to be explicitly stated.

Downloading material from the internet is a common example of making copies of potentially copyrighted content. Anyone downloading content from an online source should presume that it is copyright protected unless clearly stated otherwise.

The same rules that apply for making copies of books, printed materials, and other media for educational purposes applies to content found online. The only exception is made for posting material to the internet. This is not allowed in most cases of copyright and must be approved by the rights owner.

There are some steps people can take when posting materials online in an educational setting to stay within copyright rules. One strategy is to post the materials on a password-protected website, where only students can access what is posted. This can guarantee that the material is used for educational purposes. Furthermore, content can be distributed online using streaming technology so students cannot download the material and keep a copy on their own computers.

FILE SHARING

File swapping is when one person shares a digital file, such as an MP3, with one or more people. There are numerous ways for people to share files illegally online. File sharing became very popular in 1999 when the file-sharing system Napster was introduced. Napster connected users directly to one another. It was incredibly successful and spawned numerous programs that allowed for distributing any type of file among large numbers of people.

Napster and similar programs are known as peer-to-peer programs. The Digital Millennium Copyright Act

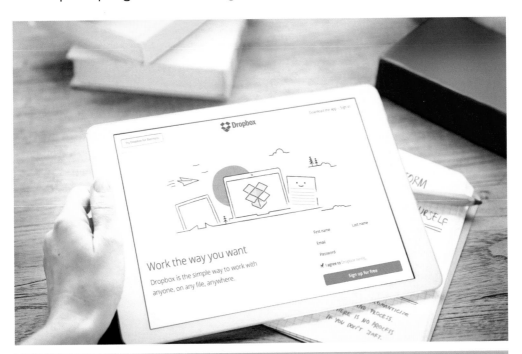

File-sharing platforms were sometimes abused in the early 2000s to share media like films and music illegally. Nowadays, platforms like Dropbox constantly develop safeguards to prevent such activity.

does not account for peer-to-peer file swapping programs. Rights owners tried to look for help from other sources, such as internet service providers (ISPs) and online search engines, to help stop file swapping. However, the DMCA does protect these companies from responsibility when their users violate copyright laws. Instead, the content industry, such as music and movie publishers, went after individual file sharers. They focused on finding those who infringed on their intellectual property and taking them to court.

Over time, media and technology companies launched services and platforms that offered legal ways to download and listen to music online and even purchase copies of music files they could then own themselves. Consumer attitudes toward the new way to listen to music changed. Services such as iTunes and Spotify became successful. Paid downloads for music increased and proved to be a better solution to fighting piracy than taking people and online companies, such as file-sharing businesses, to court. Giving consumers access to music online also proved to be more effective than restrictive technologies that many found to be problematic.

CHAPTER FIVE

FAIR USE AND RESPECTFUL BEHAVIOR

Treating digital content and media respectfully means following the many copyright rules in place. There are ways to be certain that using materials found online does not infringe on copyrights. This includes media such as books, movies, and music available on the internet.

FAIR USE

Copyrights have limitations. There are some things that people are free to do with certain digital media. Such rules fall under a doctrine known as fair use. Fair use refers to uses of copyrighted works allowed without requiring permission from the rights holder first. Many of the rights allowed in educational situations are considered fair use, such as nonprofit use in a classroom. In addition to teaching, research, and scholarship, fair use includes criticism, commentary, and news reporting. For example, a student is free to include copyrighted music or movies if it is for a critique or analysis of the work. If a book is newsworthy, a student newspaper is free to quote the work for news reporting.

There are specific requirements that must be met in order to qualify as fair use. In order to be certain that no copyrights are infringed upon in schoolwork or educational research, four factors are tested against the potentially illegal use of digital media. All four are examined and contribute to the overall judgment of fair use. Not all factors need to be met, however.

The legal system has not established clear tests for fair use. Each situation is looked at on a case-by-case basis. This makes determining fair use a difficult task.

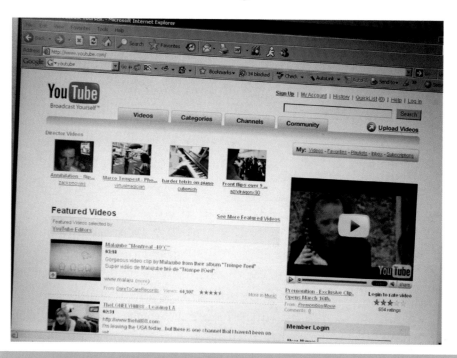

Advertising is the main way that YouTube's millions of content creators make money off the videos they post. They must adhere to specific rules to make sure they do so legally and ethically.

One noted legal mind, Judge Learned Hand, famous as one of the foremost experts and thinkers on copyright law in the twentieth century, often commented that the concept of fair use was one of the most complicated and troublesome of all.

FIRST FACTOR: PURPOSE AND CHARACTER

The first factor checked when judging if a use of copyrighted material qualifies as fair use examines the purpose and the character of the work. If the use changes or repurposes the original work in a way that adds value, then it can be considered fair use. Parody or satire falls into this category. Textbooks and other teaching materials do not fall into this category, however, as they are meant to be used for teaching.

At the same time, access to the copyrighted material must be strictly for student and researcher use and not for profit. If it is available online for anyone to use, then it is not fair use. If the purpose of using copyrighted material is to charge money for it, then it does not qualify as fair use. Anything considered as a commercial purpose would be a violation of copyright.

SECOND FACTOR: NATURE OF THE COPYRIGHTED MATERIAL

Different kinds of material receive different levels of protection. Factual or informational works do not receive as great a level of copyright protection as creative works. For example, using a song or poem does not count as fair use as often as something made up of facts, such as a graph or timeline. Similarly, unpublished works also receive greater copyright protection than published works. It is easier to have published works counted as fair use than something not officially released or published. This means that a student should be more careful when using something like an unreleased song in his or her work than a popular song that plays on the radio.

As with the first factor, if there is a commercial aspect to the new work, then it is not considered fair use. If the new work is meant to be copied, such as from a textbook or other educational source, then it has a better chance of being considered fair use. However, if it is meant to be purchased, there could be issues.

There are restrictions on what concert attendees can and cannot record and later share or sell.

THIRD FACTOR: AMOUNT USED

Yet another factor taken into account is the amount of the original work used. If the amount used is short or a small portion of the whole, such as just a few sentences out of an entire book, then it has a better chance of being seen as fair use. Students should be careful, however, because using only a small amount does not always guarantee fair use. If the content used is the "heart of the work," then it could be considered copyright infringement. Conversely, a large amount of the original work can be used if it is for educational or research purposes.

The allowable amount of a copyrighted image has differed in copyrights that have been challenged in court. Legally, smaller or lower-resolution versions of images are allowable. Smaller versions of images are commonly called thumbnails. Websites sometimes use thumbnail images as links to other web pages.

FOURTH FACTOR: EFFECT ON THE MARKET

The final factor in determining fair use is how the new work affects the market for the original work. This means that if the new work makes it harder for the original work to make money or turn a profit, then it may not be classified as fair use.

Singing "Happy Birthday" onscreen was restricted for many years, until the owners released the song to the public domain in 2016.

For example, if a student were to use a popular song in a project and it somehow affected the sales of the original song, the use would be restricted. Even if the impact is small, the courts do not take this factor lightly.

ELECTRONIC CONSIDERATIONS

The ease of copying and distributing electronic media, such as audio and video files, the quality of the work, and ease of distribution are all big factors in determining fair use. Works that can be sent or shared online can have a bigger impact on the market for the original work. Students should be careful when using digital media in their work, particularly when posting something online.

If the quality of the original work is reduced, such as when an image is downsized into a thumbnail image, then its use could be considered fair use. The court or judge must deem the new work to be transformative—that is, different enough from the original work. Making an exact copy of an original work will likely not be seen as fair use, but reducing the quality can sometimes help lower the risk of copyright infringement.

COMPLYING WITH THE LAW

The Association of Research Libraries recommends students ask themselves two questions when determining if their work violates copyright law or not. The first is, "Did you use the work in a different manner or for a

Singer Robin Thicke is shown here outside court in Los Angeles in 2015. He and musician Pharrell paid $7.2 million in damages because their song "Blurred Lines" borrowed too heavily from Marvin Gaye.

different purpose than the original?" If students do not answer yes, then it will most likely not be considered fair use.

The second question is, "Did you use an amount of the original work that is appropriate to your new, transformative purpose?" The answer here must also be yes. There are surprising ways that schoolwork can be considered transformative. According to the US Patent and Trademark Office, simply copying and distributing articles can sometimes be considered transformative in the right situation.

For students, fair use applies when accessing electronic materials either on a class website or library, submitting papers, applying for scholarships, or browsing digitized versions of unique materials. For classes that require making use of online video, such as filmmaking classes or classes on digital media, fair use will often come up. Some areas of study already have codes of best practices in place to help guide students, including those studying media, journalism, music, film, and many other disciplines.

Finally, if a professor or teacher posts material for students to use online, such as on e-reserves or sites such as Blackboard or Moodle, do not automatically assume the material is free to use. Professors may share copyrighted materials online but are barred from copying them, distributing them, or other activities protected by copyright. Having a teacher post material online does not change its copyright status for students.

CHAPTER SIX

NAVIGATING DIGITAL RIGHTS

With so many rules in place both for protecting copyright holders and people who use their work, it can be difficult to know exactly how to respect digital media found online.

AVOIDING COPYRIGHT INFRINGEMENT

Understanding how people infringe on other people's work goes a long way in helping students avoid making the same mistakes. Some common examples of copyright infringement that youth regularly encounter include:

- Downloading movies without paying for them
- Recording movies in a theater
- Using another's photos without permission
- Copying software code without giving credit
- Creating videos with unlicensed music clips
- Copying books, blogs, or podcasts without permission
- Copying any original work without permission

There are also common misconceptions about what uses are allowable. For example, some code used for programming is labeled as open source, or free to be used and distributed. However, any open source code may come with rules for commercial use. Many people believe also that using three- to five-second clips of music is acceptable. This is not always true if it is not deemed to be fair use. Finally, no matter how big a company is, or how small, they are within their rights to respond to cases of copyright infringement as they see fit.

The only way to guarantee avoiding copyright infringement is to obtain permission. The US Copyright Office has laid out steps for legally obtaining permission for using

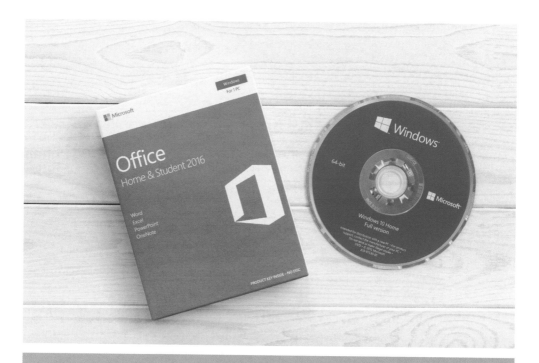

Software for sale—like the Microsoft Office suite of applications—is protected by copyright. Schools or other institutions using copies of it may be violating user agreements.

copyrighted work. It points out that, although not all unauthorized uses of copyrighted work are infringing, copyright law gives owners a variety of exclusive rights to protect their work.

FINDING THE OWNER

The Copyright Office is not responsible for granting permission to use copyrighted work. Only the copyright owner can do that. Before reaching out to obtain permission, however, it recommends that someone first research the copyright status of the work.

The work may have a copyright notice somewhere, such as on its packaging or on a book's copyright page. This notice identifies the copyright owner. However, beginning on March 1, 1989, the law changed, making the copyright notice optional. Absence of the notice, then, does not imply lack of a copyright. The copyright owner may have also changed since the original notice was created. An original work may also have its copyright belonging to a different owner from the larger work, such as the rights to a section of a book belonging to a different owner than the book itself.

In cases where there is no notice and the owner cannot be located, the Copyright Office recommends contacting the author or publisher of the work. They may be able to find or contact the current copyright owner. Otherwise, the Copyright Office should be able to find the owner. The office keeps records of registrations and transfers of ownership. For records created

Steve Herman, who runs the Library of Congress storage facility in Washington, DC, is shown here giving a tour of the space. Out of print works may still be protected, even if records are scarce.

after December 31, 1977, students can visit www
.copyright.gov, while records from before 1978 are
available at the office's physical location or at archive
.org/details/copyrightrecords.

CONTACTING THE OWNER

Since the Copyright Office cannot grant permissions,
students should contact the copyright owner directly.
Incomplete information by those requesting permissions is a common reason for a delay in responding
to requests. In order to receive permission quickly,
there are several key items students should provide
copyright owners. First, copyright owners will need to
know what specific content is being used and include
the author's, editor's, or translator's name along with
the title and other details about the work. They should
outline the exact material to be used or shared, too.
The more detail provided, such as date of copyright,
the better it is for everyone involved.

The permission seeker must also describe pre-
cisely the nature of the new project to the granter.
Important details include to whom the new work will
be made available and whether or not the new work
will be up for sale. Students should provide their full
name and contact details as well as the name of their
school, organization, or other institution and whether
it is commercial or nonprofit.

Students should contact the copyright owner as
soon as possible to allow for enough time to receive

an answer. Research is sometimes required on the copyright owner's end, which can add time as well. The copyright office maintains contact details for individual authors. Some publishers, especially larger, established ones, also have their own departments dedicated to rights and permissions. Students may be required to pay a fee for obtaining the rights to use copyrighted work, but the decision ultimately rests with the owner or owners.

USING IMAGES IN PRESENTATIONS

Students should be careful when using images researched online in their presentations. If they are unable to rely on only their own photos, then there are some things they can do to help avoid infringement. The experts recommend looking for images that are free to use in any way they please. Labels to look for include "free to share and use"; "use for commercial purposes"; "labeled for reuse"; "free to use, share, or modify, even commercially"; and "modify, adapt, or build upon"; or other similar phrasing. If an image is marked as "noncommercial use," then students should be careful to use the image for work that they will not get paid for. For example, one expert noted that although the New York Public Library made thousands of images freely available, there was language in their terms and conditions that hinted at limited use.

Online image resources include licensing requirements for all of their digital media. Experts suggest carefully reading these before using any of their

When you do your homework on copyrighted materials, you can be confident that any presentation you give has adhered to proper standards regarding content and intellectual property.

images. They recommend being cautious even in educational uses since someone could upload images from the presentation with the presenter's name on it, thus potentially infringing on the copyright.

TEACH ACT

In 2001, the US Congress passed the Technology, Education and Copyright Harmonization (TEACH) Act in response to the changing times. It helped revise and update older copyright laws that did not account for distance-learning technologies. The TEACH Act allows for limited additional protection for teachers in an e-classroom or digital environment.

With the act, new types of content were covered under existing copyright rules. The act allowed for posting materials online for a short amount of time and no longer required students to be physically in the same location as the content posted by their teachers. However, there were a number of rules put into place to protect rights holders. These restrictions and requirements are seen by educators as too strict, robbing the TEACH Act of its power.

There are also obvious images to avoid, such as a company's logo or well-known mascots and characters. Cartoonists are notably aggressive in defending their copyright claims. Students should be particularly careful to avoid using their work without proper permissions. In addition to cartoonists, the experts mention that companies that sell stock images, such as Getty Images, regularly search the internet for illegal use of their content.

RESPECTING DIGITAL RIGHTS

The US court system has specified several types of uses that are considered fair use. Quoting small parts of a work in a review for illustration, criticism, or comment or in scholarly or technical work is considered fair use. Parody, summaries, and reproductions of a legislative report or judicial proceeding are also fair use. Students are specifically given the ability to reproduce a small part of a work to illustrate a lesson.

When a student is assigned a project that requires using resources found online, the first thing to do is determine what will be needed and how the material will be used. Will the project require audio or video files? Will this be a text-only resource? Is this intended for classroom use only, or is there a possibility of making money from the project? For example, if the project deals with creating a computer program, will the program one day be sold for others to use? Digital content is easy to distribute online, so students must determine if their new project will be made available over the internet.

Once the specifics have been determined, students should consider other acceptable and legal uses of copyrighted material. These include criticism, parody, satire, and similar purposes. Outside of these specific uses, it is a good idea to apply the four factors that determine if the new use of copyrighted material qualifies as fair use.

Students should also ponder the purpose of the digital content they want to use. Next verify the nature of the work being used, such as if it is factual or fictional content. Fair use takes into account how much of the material will be used, so students should finalize how much they need for their projects. Finally, the new project's effect on the market should be evaluated.

If it does not seem that the project qualifies as fair use, the next step is to obtain permissions from the copyright holder. There are several ways to go about this, but it will take some time and effort to pinpoint the correct person or company to contact. Once the owner or owners have been found, they will then need to be contacted as soon as possible to allow for ample response time. Sometimes they will need to

When in doubt, you can usually consult a teacher, professor, or someone else well versed in intellectual-property issues to make sure you are obtaining and using digital content properly.

be contacted multiple times if they do not respond in a reasonable amount of time.

There are many layers and details when it comes to respecting digital content and media. With so many resources available online, it is easy to move forward without thinking twice about how much work was required by the creator to provide those materials. Maintaining respect for other people's work can help students avoid plagiarism and abusing the power of the internet, while creating something new in the world online and off.

ACTIVITIES

Activity 1
Identifying Legal and Ethical Content Uses
Classroom groups or individuals make up teams that hunt for content and judge whether or not it falls under fair use and other restrictions.
- One team looks up classic books from the early to mid-twentieth century.
- Another finds clips of old and newer films.
- Yet another might do internet searches for sports broadcasts and other recorded content.

Activity 2
Permissions Practice
Students in groups or individually find bits of digital media online, identify the copyright owners, and prepare letters to request permission to use the media.
- Students judge each others' letters, raising issues or providing input on how to improve or streamline these requests.
- They can look up content creators on YouTube and other sites, examining cases where recording companies and other big copyright holders have removed people's videos due to infractions and how different creators (like movie and game reviewers, for example) have dealt with these challenges.

Activity 3
Cards Against Copyright Infringement
Students form teams or play individually in a game to explore what kinds of content or uses infringe upon

copyrights, which are fair use, and which require special permission or fees.

- The larger group brainstorms dozens of cases that fall under all these categories and writes each one on the flip side of pieces of paper or cards. These are shuffled or mixed up and chosen at random, giving each player or group a set amount.
- The larger group also draws up permission approvals and denials for the applicable content types and requests. These are shuffled and given out to all players or groups. The players can establish rules for trading cards they are dealt, with the ultimate goal being to match content cards with the permissions and approvals cards that correspond to them. The first player or group that assembles a perfect hand of matches wins.

GLOSSARY

copyright The legal right to be the only one to reproduce, publish, or sell any form of artistic work.

digital media A form of media that can be read and
distributed by electronic devices.

encryption Changing information or data into code,
especially to prevent unauthorized access.

fair use Use of copyrighted works allowed without
requiring receiving permission from the rights holder.

infringement Breaking the terms of a law or agreement.

intellectual property A work or invention that is the
result of creativity to which one has rights and can
be legally protected.

legislative report Written expression of an official govern-
mental position on laws.

noncommercial Not intended for sale or profit.

open source Original source code for a computer program that is freely available and may be redistribut-
ed and modified.

parody A creative work in which the style of an author or
work is imitated for comedic effect.

patent A right of an inventor to solely make, use, or sell
his or her invention for a length of time.

piracy The use or reproduction of another person's
work without permission, in violation of patent or
copyright.

public domain Refers to the collection of works that are
free to use by the general public without payment or
permission being required.

secure container A form of encryption technology that

makes certain forms of digital media inaccessible to those without authorization.

stream To transmit or receive data, video, or audio material over the internet as a continuous flow.

thumbnail A small computer graphic, often a version of a larger file or separate internet site or page, often placed to represent a link one can click on to get to that larger file or location.

trademark A symbol, word, or words legally registered by use as representing a company or product.

transformative Describing something that causes a big change in something

verification A process establishing the truth, accuracy, or validity of something.

satire A creative work that makes fun of and shows the weaknesses of human nature.

FOR MORE INFORMATION

Access Copyright
320-56 Wellesley Street West
Toronto, ON M5S 2S3
Canada
(800) 893-5777
Email: info@accesscopyright.ca
Website: http://www.accesscopyright.ca
Access Copyright represents Canadian writers, artists,
    publishers, and licensees in the copying of their work
    to educational organizations, businesses, and more.

Canadian Intellectual Property Office
Place du Portage I
50 Victoria Street, Room C-229
Gatineau, QC K1A 0C9
(866) 997-1936
Website: http://www.ic.gc.ca/eic/site/cipointernet
    -internetopic.nsf/eng/h_wr00003.html
Twitter: @CIPO_Canada
The Canadian Intellectual Property Office (CIPO) over-
    sees intellectual property in Canada as well as pat-
    ents, trademarks, copyrights, industrial designs, and
    integrated circuit topographies

CommCopyright Society of the USA
1 East 53rd Street, Floor 8
New York, NY 10022
(212) 354-6401
Website: http://www.csusa.org
Facebook and Twitter: @thecsusa

The Copyright Society of the USA is a nonprofit organization that helps people understand copyright law
and interact with others in the field.

Common Sense Media
650 Townsend, Suite 435
San Francisco, CA 94103
(415) 863-0600
Website: https://www.commonsensemedia.org
This nonprofit organization has made it its mission to
help kids navigate and thrive in the digital environment. They provide unbiased information, advice,
and innovative tools to help parents and educators
use the power of media and technology as a force
for good in kids' lives.

Landmarks for Schools
PO Box 19637
Raleigh, NC 27619
(919) 571-3292
Website: http://www.landmark-project.com
Landmarks for Schools provides information for students regarding digital resources found online. The
website provides a free copyright permission request template.

Library of Congress (LOC)
101 Independence Avenue SE
Washington, DC 20540
(202) 707-5000
Website: http://www.loc.gov

Facebook: @libraryofcongress

Instagram and Twitter: @librarycongress

The Library of Congress, the largest library in the world, serves as a research institution not just for the US government, but for scholars worldwide.

US Copyright Office

101 Independence Avenue SE

Washington, DC 20559

(877) 476–0778

Website: http://www.copyright.gov

Twitter: @copyrightoffice

YouTube: @uscopyrightoffice

The United States Copyright Office administers the complicated copyright regulations, provides services that include registration and record keeping, and provides advice to lawmaking and administrative bodies of the federal government regarding copyright.

FOR FURTHER READING

Berlatsky, Noah. *Netiquette and Online Ethics*. Detroit, MI: Greenhaven Press, 2013.

Fisk, Nathan W. *Digital Piracy*. New York, NY: Chelsea House, 2011.

Fromm, Megan. *Ethics and Digital Citizenship*. New York, NY: Rosen Publishing, 2015.

Gould, Sloane. *Online Rights and Responsibilities: Digital Citizenship*. New York, NY: PowerKids Press, 2018.

Laine, Carolee, and Brandy Karl. *Content Ownership and Copyright*. Minneapolis, MN: Abdo Publishing, 2017.

Meyer, Susan. *Understanding Digital Piracy*. New York, NY: Rosen Publishing, 2014.

Michalski, Pete, and Henrietta M. Lily. *Research Project Success Using Digital Tools*. New York, NY: Rosen Publishing, 2016.

Popek, Emily. *Copyright and Digital Ethics*. New York, NY: Rosen Publishing, 2011.

Porterfield, Jason. *File Sharing: Rights and Risks*. New York, NY: Rosen Publishing, 2015.

Rabbat, Suzy. *Citing Sources: Learning to Use the Copyright Page*. Ann Arbor, MI: Cherry Lake Publishing, 2013.

Sinha, Manoj Kumar, and Vandana Mahalwar. *Copyright Law in the Digital World, Challenges and Opportunities*. Singapore: Springer, 2017.

BIBLIOGRAPHY

Becker, Eberhard. *Digital Rights Management: Technological, Economic, and Legal and Political Aspects*. New York, NY: Springer, 2003.

Brandom, Russell. "Woe Betide Those Who Violate Grumpy Cat's intellectual Property." The Verge, January 28, 2018. https://www.theverge .com/2018/1/28/16934202/grumpy-cat -grumppucino-trademark-lawsuit-meme.

Carlisle, Stephen. "Copyrights Last Too Long! They Don't; and Why It's Not Changing." Office of Copyright, July 23, 2014. http://copyright.nova.edu /copyright-duration.

Cheng, Jacqui. "Five Examples of Lame DMCA Takedowns." Ars Technica, May 16, 2010. https://arstechnica.com/tech-policy/2010/05 /five-examples-of-lame-dmca-takedowns.

Conn, Kathleen. *Internet and the Law: What Educators Need to Know*. Alexandria, VA: Association for Supervision & Curriculum Development, 2002.

Cox, Joseph. "Flight Simulator Add-On Tried to Catch Pirates By Installing Password-Stealing Malware on Their Computers." Motherboard, February 19, 2018. https://motherboard.vice.com/en_us/article/pamzqk /fs-labs-flight-simulator-password-malware-drm.

Garbis, Anastasios. "Tips To Help Avoid YouTube Copyright Infringement." *Law Technology Today*, March 11, 2016. http://www.lawtechnologytoday .org/2016/03/tips-avoid-copyright-infringment.

Gardner, Eriq. "Redbox Demands Disney Lose Right

to Enforce Movie Copyrights." *Hollywood Reporter*, January 26, 2018. https://www.hollywoodreporter .com/thr-esq/iredbox-demands-disney-lose-right -enforce-movie-copyrights-1078845.

Gardner, Eriq. "Warner Music Pays $14 Million to End 'Happy Birthday' Copyright Lawsuit." *Hollywood Reporter*, February 9, 2016. https://www.hollywoodreporter.com/thr-esq /warner-music-pays-14-million-863120.

Gil, Paul. "What Is 'DRM'? Why Is DRM So Controversial with Music and Movie Artists?" Lifewire, August 31, 2017. https://www.lifewire.com/why-is-drm-so -controversial-2483185.

Guardian. "The Statute of Anne." August 6, 2007. https://www.theguardian.com/technology/2007 /aug/06/statuteofanne.

Instagram Help Center. "Copyright." Retrieved March 31, 2018. https://help.instagram .com/126382350847838.

Juetten, Mary. "How to Avoid Copyright Infringement." Legalzoom.com, December 2015. https://www.legalzoom.com/articles/how-to -avoid-copyright-infringement.

Law Technology Today. "Finding Graphics, Photos, Art and Videos for Presentations." May 31, 2017. http:// www.lawtechnologytoday.org/2017/05 /finding-graphics-for-presentations.

LII Staff. "Intellectual property." LII/Legal Information Institute, August 6, 2007. https://www.law.cornell .edu/wex/intellectual_property.

Lucchi, Nicola. *Digital Media & Intellectual Property*.

New York, NY: Springer-Verlag Berlin Heidelberg, 2006.

McDonald, Steven. "Copyright Guidelines for Showing Movies and Other Audiovisual Works." Washington and Lee University. Retrieved March 7, 2018. https://www.wlu.edu/general-counsel/answer-center/copyright-and-intellectual-property/copyright-guidelines-for-showing-movies-and-other-audiovisual-works.

McGeveran, William, and William W. Fisher. "The Digital Learning Challenge: Obstacles to Educational Uses of Copyrighted Material in the Digital Age." *SSRN Electronic Journal*, 2006.

National Research Council. *The Digital Dilemma: Intellectual Property in the Information Age.* Washington, DC: National Academy Press, 2000.

New York University. "Educational and Research Uses of Copyrighted Materials Policy Statement." January 6, 2014. https://www.nyu.edu/about/policies-guidelines-compliance/policies-and-guidelines/educational-and-research-uses-of-copyrighted-materials-policy-st.html.

Pollard, Nathan. "Professor's Lecture Notes, Textbooks Copyrightable, But Fair Use Issues Remain." Bloomberg Bureau of National Affairs, December 3, 2010. https://www.bna.com/professors-lecture-notes-n6469.

Smith, Richard. "What Is Digital Media?" The Centre for Digital Media, October 15, 2013. https://thecdm.ca/news/faculty-news/2013/10/15/what-is-digital-media.

Stim, Richard. "Educational Uses of Non-coursepack Materials." Stanford University Libraries, April 17, 2017. https://fairuse.stanford.edu/overview /academic-and-educational-permissions /non-coursepack.

Stim, Richard. *Patent, Copyright & Trademark: an Intellectual Property Desk Reference.* Berkeley, CA: Nolo, 2018.

University of California. "Copyright in the Classroom." Retrieved March 29, 2018. http://copyright .universityofcalifornia.edu/use/teaching.html.

Washington State University "The Internet & Copyright." Retrieved March 20, 2018. https://ucomm.wsu.edu /the-internet-copyright.

INDEX

ABOUT THE AUTHOR

Jeff Mapua is the author of several books focusing on technology and the internet, including *Net Neutrality and What It Means to You, Making the Most of Crowdfunding*, and *A Career in Customer Service and Tech Support.* Mapua's professional career is in web-based technology and websites for international corporations. Mapua lives in Chicago with his wife, Ruby, and their bulldog, Daisy.

PHOTO CREDITS

Cover, p. 15 Hero Images/Getty Images; cover, back cover, and interior pages background (abstract) Toria/Shutterstock.com; cover, p. 3 (icons) pluie_r/Shutterstock.com; p. 5 Klaus Vedfelt/DigitalVision/Getty Images; p. 8 VW Pics/Universal Images Group/Getty Images; p. 10 Dean Drobot /Shutterstock.com; p. 13 Denys Prykhodov/Shutterstock.com; p. 16 Bloomberg/Getty Images; p. 18 Library of Congress, Rare Book and Special Collections Division; p. 21 Grisha Bruev/Shutterstock.com; p. 23 Ermolaev Alexander/Shutterstock.com; p. 27 Sylv1rob1/Shutterstock .com; p. 29 Murat Kucukkarakasli/Shutterstock.com; p. 30 Ariel Skelley /DigitalVision/Getty Images; p. 32 © iStockphoto.com/Ferlistockphoto; p. 37 Martyn Goddard/Corbis Documentary/Getty Images; p. 38 Bloomberg/Getty Images; p. 41 Jetta Productions/Blend Images/ Getty Images; p. 43 Rawpixel.com/Shutterstock.com; p. 46 Robert Sullivan/AFP/Getty Images; p. 48 Dusan Petkovic/Shutterstock.com; p. 49 Wavebreakmedia/Shutterstock.com; p. 51 David Buchan/Getty Images; p. 54 Nor Gal/Shutterstock.com; p. 56 © AP Images; p. 59 Noel Hendrickson/Photographer's Choice/Getty Images; p. 62 © iStockphoto .com/DGLimages.

Design: Michael Moy; Editor: Philip Wolny; Photo Researcher: Sherri Jackson